NLP Techniques in Personal Finance and Wealth Management

By Rex Morton

NLP Techniques in Personal Finance and Wealth Management

Copyright Page

© 2023 by Rex Morton

This book is a work of non-fiction. Unless otherwise noted, the author and the publisher make no explicit guarantees as to the accuracy of the information contained in this book and will not be held responsible for any errors or omissions.

Published by Omniterra Media Inc

First Edition

Visit the author's website at www.rexmorton.com

For information regarding special discounts for bulk purchases, please contact Rex Morton @ Rex@rexmorton.com.

Disclaimer

This book is intended to provide information about the fields of Neuro-Linguistic Programming (NLP) and Cognitive Behavioural Therapy (CBT) and their potential integration. While the author has made every effort to ensure that the information was correct at the time of publication, the author does not assume and hereby disclaims any liability to any party for any loss, damage, or disruption caused by errors or omissions, whether such errors or omissions result from negligence, accident, or any other cause.

The contents of this book should not be used as a substitute for professional advice, diagnosis, or treatment. The reader should always consult with a qualified healthcare provider about any mental health concerns or conditions. Never disregard professional psychological or medical advice or delay in seeking it because of something you have read in this book.

The views expressed in this work are solely those of the author and do not necessarily reflect the views of the publisher, and the publisher hereby disclaims any responsibility for them.

The inclusion of websites, links, or references to other resources does not mean that the author or the publisher endorses the information the organization or website may provide or recommendations it might make. Furthermore, the author does not guarantee the accuracy of the information these resources provide.

The use of any information provided in this book is solely at your own risk.

1.1 Explanation of the Book's Purpose and Objectives

Welcome to an exploration of two fascinating and powerful fields - Neuro-Linguistic Programming (NLP) and Personal Finance and Wealth Management. The purpose of this book is to unveil the connection between these two areas and provide you with the tools and techniques to leverage this intersection for your own financial health and prosperity.

The objective is not merely to educate you about these fields but to empower you to apply the principles and techniques to your own life. We aim to help you harness the power of NLP to improve your financial mindset, make better financial decisions, and, ultimately, increase your wealth and financial well-being. Whether you're a financial novice or an experienced investor, there are insights and techniques in this book that can benefit you.

1.2 Overview of Neuro-Linguistic Programming (NLP)

Neuro-Linguistic Programming is an approach that employs successful people's strategies and methods to achieve a personal objective. It links the acquired concepts, language, and behaviour patterns to specific outcomes.

NLP was developed in the 1970s by Richard Bandler and John Grinder, who believed that if the effective patterns of behaviour of exceptional people could be modeled, then these patterns could be acquired by others. NLP uses perceptual, behavioural, and communication techniques to make it easier to change thoughts and actions.

In short, NLP is about understanding how we think, communicate and behave, and using that understanding to make positive changes and achieve our goals. The techniques and methodologies of NLP are applicable in many areas of life, including personal development, education, business, and, as we will explore in this book, personal finance and wealth management.

1.3 Overview of Personal Finance and Wealth Management

Personal finance is the management of individual or family financial activities, including income generation, spending, saving, investing, and protection against risks. It involves planning for short-term and long-term financial needs and implementing those plans. Key areas of personal finance include budgeting, managing debts, investing for the future, and planning for retirement.

Wealth management, on the other hand, is a more holistic approach to managing one's financial life. It goes beyond regular financial planning and investment management. Wealth management involves creating a diversified investment portfolio, planning for your estate, managing tax liability, and more. It's about maximizing your wealth and ensuring it serves your life goals.

This book aims to help you understand and apply NLP techniques to these areas of personal finance and wealth management. It's about equipping you with the psychological tools to change your financial mindset, make smarter financial decisions, and manage your wealth more effectively.

As we journey through the chapters of this book, we will delve deeper into these fields, exploring their intersection, and providing practical tips, techniques, and case studies. We hope you find the journey enlightening and empowering.

Remember, the goal is not just to learn, but to change. To not only understand the principles and techniques discussed but to apply them. Because knowledge is not power until it's applied.

So let's begin this journey together, towards financial well-being and prosperity.

Chapter 2: Neuro-Linguistic Programming: A Primer

2.1 History and Development of Neuro-Linguistic Programming

The birth of NLP: The inception and initial goals

Richard Bandler and John Grinder: The founding fathers

Influences: The prominent figures and theories that shaped NLP

Key milestones in the evolution of NLP

The development of key concepts and models

Expansion of NLP: From therapy to personal development, business, and beyond

NLP today: Current trends and applications

2.2 Basic Principles and Assumptions of Neuro-Linguistic Programming

The NLP Presuppositions: The fundamental assumptions that guide NLP practice

The map is not the territory: Understanding subjective experience.

The power of positive intent: Assuming every behaviour has a positive intention.

The mind and body are interconnected: The role of physiology in state and behaviour.

Others including: The law of requisite variety, the feedback vs failure concept, etc.

The pillars of NLP: Relationship building, sensory awareness, a focus on outcomes, and behavioural adaptability.

The role of the unconscious mind in NLP.

2.3 Core Techniques and Methodologies in Neuro-Linguistic Programming

NLP Modeling: The process of recreating excellence Unconscious assimilation and conscious understanding Coding and transferring the model.

Representational Systems and Submodalities: How we represent and manipulate our internal world Visual, auditory, kinesthetic, olfactory, and gustatory systems.

The power of submodalities in changing beliefs and states NLP Techniques for Change:

Anchoring: Creating and utilizing powerful emotional states Swish patterns, Visual-Kinesthetic Disassociation, and other techniques for managing states and overcoming issues.

Meta-model and Milton model: Enhancing communication and influencing change.

By the end of this book, you should have a strong foundational understanding of NLP, ready to apply these concepts in the context of personal finance and wealth management.

3.1 Understanding Money and Finance

Money is a tool of exchange, used to pay for goods and services. It is an essential part of our daily lives, facilitating trade and enabling us to plan for the future. Money can be seen as a store of value, allowing us to save and defer consumption until a later date.

Understanding the basics of personal finance is essential for financial well-being. This includes understanding income (your earnings from work or investments), expenses (what you spend on living costs and lifestyle choices), savings (money set aside for future use or emergencies), and investments (assets purchased with the hope of generating income or appreciation in the future).

Financial literacy also involves understanding key concepts such as interest, inflation, risk and return, and the time value of money. For example, interest is the cost of borrowing money or the income from lending it. Inflation erodes the value of money over time, whereas the time value of money concept implies that money available now is more valuable than the same amount in the future due to its earning potential.

Money also has a psychological aspect, tied to our emotions, beliefs, and behaviours. Our money mindset can greatly influence our financial decisions and outcomes.

3.2 Key Concepts in Wealth Management

Wealth management goes beyond just financial planning. It is a holistic approach to managing an individual's financial life, including assets, liabilities, and plans for the future.

Key elements of wealth management include asset management (the process of investing and managing a portfolio of assets), estate planning (preparing for the transfer of wealth upon death), tax planning (strategies to minimize tax liability), risk management (identifying and managing potential financial risks), and retirement planning (planning for financial security in retirement).

Diversification is a crucial concept in wealth management. By spreading investments across different types of assets (like stocks, bonds, and real estate), you can potentially reduce risk and enhance returns.

Setting clear financial goals is essential, and a personal financial plan can serve as a roadmap to achieving these goals. Sometimes, professional help from financial advisors may be beneficial in managing your wealth effectively.

3.3 Common Challenges and Issues in Personal Finance

Personal finance comes with its own set of challenges. Common financial mistakes include not having a budget, accumulating high-interest debt, not saving or investing for the future, and not having an emergency fund.

Understanding debt is crucial. Not all debt is bad, but high-interest debt (like credit card debt) can quickly become a burden. Conversely, "good" debt (like a mortgage or student loans) is an investment that can pay off in the future.

Another challenge is saving and investing for retirement. With increasing life expectancies and rising costs, planning for retirement is more important than ever.

Unforeseen financial emergencies and unexpected expenses can also pose challenges. Having an emergency fund can provide a financial safety net in these situations.

In the next chapters, we will delve into how Neuro-Linguistic Programming (NLP) can help address these issues and enhance your personal finance and wealth management skills.

4.1 Overview of how Neuro-Linguistic Programming can be applied to personal finance

Neuro-Linguistic Programming (NLP) can be considered a powerful tool for molding behaviour and thought patterns. Its application in personal finance is no less significant. By addressing one's perceptions and attitudes towards money, NLP helps in reshaping financial behaviours and decision-making processes. The approach involves different elements of NLP, such as modeling, reframing, anchoring, and meta-programs, to name a few.

Modeling, for instance, is one of the key methodologies in NLP. This involves observing and replicating the successful behaviours of individuals who have attained financial success. By analyzing their attitudes, beliefs, and strategies, we can incorporate these successful traits into our own financial behaviour. This can range from investing wisely, saving efficiently, to managing debts effectively.

Reframing is another key technique in NLP. It is used to change the meaning of our perceptions or experiences to create a different emotional response. In the context of personal finance, reframing can help to alter our perception of money and wealth, which can positively impact our financial decisions and behaviours.

Anchoring, on the other hand, involves associating a specific emotional state or response with a unique trigger or 'anchor'. This can be used to develop a positive emotional response towards financial tasks that might otherwise be seen as tedious or stressful, such as budgeting, investing, or saving.

Meta-programs, finally, are deeply ingrained patterns of thought that influence our reactions and decision-making processes. Understanding and adjusting these patterns can lead to significant changes in our financial behaviour.

4.2 Case studies of successful application of Neuro-Linguistic Programming in personal finance

Case Study 1: The Power of Reframing in Debt Management Consider the case of a client struggling with high levels of credit card debt. The client viewed debt as a tremendous burden and felt overwhelmed and helpless. Through the application of NLP techniques, specifically reframing, the practitioner helped the client view the debt not as a burden, but as a challenge to be overcome. This shift in perception empowered the client to take proactive steps towards managing and eventually eliminating the debt.

Case Study 2: Modeling for Successful Investment Strategies Another case study involves a client who was hesitant to invest due to fear of risk. The NLP practitioner introduced the client to the modeling technique. They studied the behaviours, strategies, and attitudes of successful investors. The client then began to incorporate these traits, leading to a more confident and informed approach to investing. The outcome was a more diverse and robust investment portfolio, and an improved attitude towards risk and reward.

These case studies highlight how NLP techniques can be instrumental in reshaping one's financial behaviours and decision-making processes. By harnessing the power of NLP, individuals can overcome financial challenges and work towards a prosperous financial future.

5.1 Using Neuro-Linguistic Programming for belief change about money

Neuro-Linguistic Programming (NLP) can be a powerful tool in changing our beliefs about money. Our beliefs, whether positive or negative, have a profound impact on our financial behaviours and decisions.

For example, a person may hold a belief that money is the root of all evil. This negative belief may lead to self-sabotage, such as avoiding opportunities to earn more or making poor financial decisions. By using NLP, we can identify and challenge this belief.

An NLP technique called reframing can be instrumental in this process. Reframing involves changing the way we perceive a particular belief or situation. In this case, the negative belief about money can be reframed to something more positive, such as "money is a tool that can provide security and opportunities." This positive reframe can lead to more constructive financial behaviours and decisions.

5.2 Neuro-Linguistic Programming techniques for goal setting and financial planning

Setting financial goals is a key aspect of successful wealth management. However, many people find this process challenging. NLP offers techniques that can make goal setting more effective and motivating.

An NLP technique known as the Well-Formed Outcome is particularly effective for goal setting. This technique involves defining the goal in specific, positive, and achievable terms, envisioning the outcome, identifying resources needed, and considering the impact of achieving the goal on other areas of life.

For instance, a person may have a vague goal of wanting to save more money. Using the Well-Formed Outcome technique, this goal can be transformed into a more specific and motivating one, such as "I want to save $10,000 in a year for a down payment on a house. I will do this by setting aside $834 each month, cutting down on non-essential expenses, and taking on additional freelance work. Achieving this goal will bring me closer to owning my own home and will increase my financial stability."

5.3 Neuro-Linguistic Programming for overcoming financial fears and anxieties

Financial fears and anxieties can be significant barriers to effective wealth management. Fear of financial loss, anxiety about investing, or stress over debt can all lead to poor financial decisions. NLP provides techniques to address and overcome these fears and anxieties.

One such technique is known as anchoring. Anchoring involves creating a mental association between a positive emotional state and a specific trigger or 'anchor.' For example, a person may feel anxious about checking their bank account. Using the anchoring technique, they can create an association between a positive emotion, such as calmness or confidence, and the act of checking their bank account.

To create this anchor, the person can recall a time when they felt calm and confident, vividly remembering the details of the experience. While in this positive emotional state, they can create a unique physical gesture, such as tapping their fingers together. With repetition, the person can use this gesture as an 'anchor' to trigger the positive emotional state whenever they feel anxious about their finances.

By using NLP techniques like reframing, the Well-Formed Outcome, and anchoring, individuals can improve their financial mindset, leading to more effective financial decision-making and wealth management.

6.1 Applying Neuro-Linguistic Programming techniques for better financial decision making

Making sound financial decisions is a critical aspect of wealth management. NLP can help enhance this skill through its techniques such as modeling and perceptual positions.

Modeling is an NLP technique where we study and replicate the behaviours, strategies, and thought patterns of successful individuals. For instance, if someone is particularly adept at making investment decisions, you can model their approach. This could include studying how they research potential investments, their risk assessment strategies, and their decision-making process. By adopting these traits, you can improve your own financial decision-making skills.

Perceptual positions is another NLP technique that can enhance decision-making. This technique involves viewing a situation from different perspectives. For instance, before making a financial decision, you can view the situation from your own perspective (first position), from the perspective of another person involved (second position), and from an objective, detached viewpoint (third position). This allows you to gain a holistic understanding of the situation and make a more informed decision.

6.2 Using Neuro-Linguistic Programming for improving negotiation and communication skills in financial contexts

Negotiation and communication skills are vital in many financial contexts, such as negotiating a salary raise, discussing terms with a financial advisor, or bargaining a price. NLP offers several techniques to improve these skills.

The concept of rapport in NLP is particularly useful for negotiation and communication. Rapport involves creating a sense of understanding and trust with the other person. This can be achieved through matching or mirroring the other person's body language, tone of voice, and language patterns. By building rapport, you can enhance your ability to influence and persuade in financial negotiations.

6.3 Leveraging Neuro-Linguistic Programming for enhancing financial discipline and habit building

Building financial discipline and cultivating positive financial habits are key to effective wealth management. NLP can be used to develop these skills through techniques such as anchoring and reframing.

Anchoring, as discussed earlier, involves associating a positive emotional state with a specific trigger or 'anchor'. This can be used to build financial discipline. For example, if you struggle to maintain a budget, you can create an anchor that associates a positive emotional state with the act of budgeting. This can make the process more enjoyable and increase your discipline in sticking to your budget.

Reframing, on the other hand, can be used to cultivate positive financial habits. For instance, if you view saving money as a sacrifice or deprivation, you can reframe this perception to view saving as a step towards financial freedom and security. This positive reframe can motivate you to cultivate the habit of saving regularly.

In summary, NLP offers a range of techniques that can enhance your wealth management skills, from decision making to negotiation, communication, financial discipline, and habit building. By applying these techniques, you can take control of your finances and move towards your financial goals.

7.1 Detailed case studies of individuals who successfully used NLP techniques to improve their financial situation

Case Study 1: Overcoming Debt through Reframing

Jane had accumulated a significant amount of debt due to poor financial decisions in her early twenties. The debt weighed heavily on her mind, causing stress and anxiety. Through the use of NLP, specifically reframing, Jane was able to alter her perception of her debt. Instead of seeing it as a burden, she began to see it as a challenge that she was capable of overcoming. This shift in mindset empowered her to take control of her finances, devise a comprehensive debt repayment plan, and eventually become debt-free.

Case Study 2: Increasing Savings through Anchoring

John always found it difficult to save money. He enjoyed living in the moment and spending on experiences and items that brought him immediate joy. However, he realized that this habit was preventing him from building a financial safety net. John started using the NLP technique of anchoring. He created a positive emotional association with the act of saving. Each time he transferred money to his savings account, he would perform his chosen anchor, which was a fist pump. Over time, John began to find satisfaction in saving, leading to a substantial increase in his savings.

7.2 Examples of how financial professionals use NLP in their practices

Financial professionals, such as financial advisors and wealth managers, often use NLP techniques to improve their services. For instance, they may use rapport building to create strong relationships with their clients, understanding their clients' financial goals and concerns on a deeper level.

Consider a financial advisor, Lisa. She uses the NLP technique of modeling to guide her clients. Lisa studies successful investors and their habits, strategies, and mindset. She then shares these insights with her clients, helping them adopt successful financial behaviours.

7.3 Practical exercises and applications for readers to try

For readers looking to apply NLP techniques to their own financial situations, here are some practical exercises:

Reframing Exercise: Identify a negative belief you have about money or finance. Write down how this belief is affecting your financial decisions. Now, try to reframe this belief into a positive one. How does this new belief change your perspective on your financial decisions?

Anchoring Exercise: Think about a financial task you find difficult or stressful, such as budgeting or saving. Now, recall a time when you felt particularly confident or happy. Immerse yourself in this memory. Create a unique physical gesture or 'anchor' to associate with this positive emotional state. Use this anchor next time you perform the financial task.

Modeling Exercise: Identify a financially successful person you admire. This could be a celebrity, a successful entrepreneur, or even someone in your personal life. Study their financial habits, attitudes, and strategies. Try to incorporate these traits into your own financial behaviour.

Through these exercises, readers can apply NLP techniques to their own financial situations, leading to improved financial behaviours and decisions.

While Neuro-Linguistic Programming (NLP) can be a powerful tool for personal development and improving financial behaviours, it is not without its challenges and critiques. Understanding these can help in making an informed decision about employing NLP techniques and setting realistic expectations about their effects.

8.1 Scientific Validity of NLP

One of the main criticisms of NLP is the lack of rigorous scientific evidence supporting its effectiveness. While many practitioners and users of NLP report positive results, these are often based on anecdotal evidence and personal testimonials. In the scientific community, NLP has not been studied extensively.

8.2 Misuse and Misrepresentation of NLP

Another critique is that NLP can be misused or misrepresented by individuals or organizations with ulterior motives. For example, some financial scams have been known to use NLP techniques to manipulate individuals into making poor financial decisions. This highlights the importance of using NLP ethically

and responsibly, and being aware of how these techniques can
be used manipulatively.

8.3 Overemphasis on Individual Responsibility

A third critique is that NLP, like many self-help methodologies,
may overemphasize individual responsibility at the expense of
recognizing external factors. While it's true that our beliefs and
behaviours play a significant role in our financial situation, they
are not the only factors. Socioeconomic conditions, systemic
issues, and unexpected life events can also have a profound
impact on our financial health. An approach that focuses solely
on changing individual beliefs and behaviours may not be
sufficient to address these broader issues.

8.4 Implementing NLP Techniques

Finally, implementing NLP techniques can be challenging. These
techniques often require a high degree of self-awareness and
discipline to apply effectively. It can also be difficult to maintain
the consistency needed to see long-term results. Moreover,
some people may find certain NLP techniques, such as modeling
or reframing, unnatural or uncomfortable.

In conclusion, while NLP can be a valuable tool for improving financial behaviours, it's important to approach it with a critical mindset, understanding its limitations and potential challenges. The most effective approach to financial health is likely to be a holistic one that combines NLP techniques with other strategies, and that acknowledges the influence of both internal and external factors.

The intersection of Neuro-Linguistic Programming (NLP) and personal finance is a relatively new and evolving field. As we look towards the future, there are many exciting possibilities and emerging trends to explore.

9.1 Exploration of emerging trends in Neuro-Linguistic Programming and personal finance

In recent years, we have seen a growing interest in the use of NLP in personal finance. This trend is driven by a broader societal shift towards financial literacy and self-improvement. People are increasingly recognizing the importance of not just understanding financial concepts, but also managing their mindset and behaviours around money.

One emerging trend is the use of NLP in financial coaching. Financial coaches use NLP techniques to help clients overcome limiting beliefs, set financial goals, and develop positive financial behaviours. This personalized approach to financial education has the potential to make a significant impact on individuals' financial health.

Another trend is the integration of NLP with technology. For example, some personal finance apps and tools are incorporating NLP techniques to help users improve their financial behaviours. This integration of NLP and technology has the potential to make these techniques more accessible and easy to apply.

9.2 Discussion of potential future developments in this field

As we look to the future, there are several potential developments that could further enhance the role of NLP in personal finance and wealth management.

One potential development is the increased use of AI and machine learning in the application of NLP techniques. For example, AI could be used to personalize NLP techniques based on individual's specific financial behaviours and goals. This could make these techniques even more effective in helping individuals improve their financial situation.

Additionally, we may see more research into the effectiveness of NLP in personal finance. This could help address some of the critiques of NLP and provide more evidence-based guidance on how to best apply these techniques.

9.3 Final thoughts and encouragement for readers to continue exploring and applying these concepts in their lives

As we conclude this exploration of Neuro-Linguistic Programming in personal finance and wealth management, it's important to remember that this is a journey, not a destination. Financial health, like physical health, is something to be nurtured and maintained over time.

The concepts and techniques discussed in this book provide a foundation, but there is always more to learn. The field of NLP is constantly evolving, and new strategies and techniques are being developed all the time.

Therefore, I encourage you, the reader, to continue exploring these concepts and applying them in your life. Experiment with different techniques, continue learning, and most importantly, remain open to growth and change. Your financial health is in your hands, and with the right tools and mindset, you have the power to shape it for the better.

As we move into the future, the intersection of Neuro-Linguistic Programming and personal finance holds great promise. By leveraging these tools and techniques, we can empower individuals to take control of their financial futures, leading to greater financial security and well-being for all.

Chapter 10: Conclusion

As we come to the end of this journey exploring the intersection of Neuro-Linguistic Programming (NLP) and personal finance, let's take a moment to reflect on the key points we've covered and the path ahead.

10.1 Recap of the key points discussed in the book

We began our exploration by understanding the fundamentals of Neuro-Linguistic Programming and personal finance. We delved into the history, basic principles, and core techniques of NLP and discussed key concepts and common challenges in personal finance.

We then examined how NLP can be applied to personal finance, with a focus on improving financial mindset and enhancing wealth management skills. We discussed various NLP techniques such as reframing, anchoring, and modeling, and how they can be used to change beliefs about money, set financial goals, overcome financial fears, make better financial decisions, improve negotiation and communication skills in financial contexts, and build financial discipline.

Through detailed case studies and practical exercises, we saw how individuals have successfully used NLP techniques to improve their financial situations and how financial professionals are incorporating NLP into their practices.

However, we also addressed the challenges and critiques of NLP, emphasizing the need for a critical mindset and a balanced approach that considers both individual behaviours and external factors.

10.2 Final thoughts and encouragement for readers to apply the techniques discussed

The power of NLP lies in its practicality. The techniques discussed in this book are not merely theoretical concepts but are tools that you can apply in your life to improve your financial health. Remember, change doesn't happen overnight. It requires consistent effort and perseverance. You will begin to see changes in your financial behaviours and mindset over time if you start modest and practice regularly.

10.3 Resources for further learning and exploration

To continue your learning journey, consider the following resources:

NLP Books: You can go to www.rexmorton.com to find many more books on the topics. I covery nearly every aspect of life as it pertains to NLP practices.

Financial Literacy Books: Enhance your understanding of personal finance with books like "The Total Money Makeover" by Dave Ramsey and "Your Money or Your Life" by Vicki Robin.

Financial Coach or NLP Practitioner: Consider working with a professional who can provide personalized guidance and support.

Remember, the journey to financial health and wealth is a lifelong one, and there's always more to learn. Keep exploring, stay curious, and continue to grow. Your financial future is in your hands.

Rex Morton is a renowned author and researcher in the United Kingdom with a passionate interest in the human mind, specifically in Cognitive Behavioural Therapy (CBT) and Neuro-Linguistic Programming (NLP).

Morton has spent a considerable portion of his professional life diving deep into the theories and principles that form the backbone of these two compelling fields. His fascination with NLP led him to complete an extensive certification program, solidifying his understanding of this innovative approach to understanding human behaviour.

Although Morton does not have clinical experience, his intense curiosity and dedication to studying these subjects have made him a respected figure in the field. He has thoroughly researched the integration of NLP techniques into CBT, offering fresh perspectives and insights into how these two methodologies can complement each other to enhance understanding of human cognition and behaviour.

As an author, Morton has successfully communicated his knowledge and passion to a broader audience, making complex psychological theories accessible to professionals and interested laypersons. His writing is characterized by a clear, engaging style and a focus on the practical application of theories, making them relevant to everyday life.

In his personal life, Morton is an ardent lover of the natural world, often spending his free time exploring the British countryside. His passion for landscape photography allows him to capture and share the beauty of these excursions. Despite his accomplishments, Morton is known for his humility and eagerness to continue learning. His work continues to inspire those interested in the intricate workings of the human mind and the exciting possibilities presented by the integration of NLP and CBT.

If you've found the content of this book enlightening and wish to continue your journey of understanding the human mind, I warmly invite you to visit my website at www.rexmorton.com. The website serves as a hub of knowledge where I share my latest findings, thoughts, and insights on the integration of NLP and CBT.

I also encourage you to subscribe to the newsletter available on the website. By subscribing, you'll receive regular updates on a range of topics, from detailed discussions on specific NLP techniques and their application in CBT, to the latest research in the field.

The newsletter is also the first place I'll share news of upcoming releases. Whether it's the announcement of a new book, the launch of an online course, newsletter subscribers will be the first to know. This is a great opportunity to continue learning directly from me, deepening your understanding of NLP and CBT, and enhancing your skills in applying these techniques in your own life or professional practice.

I'm looking forward to sharing this journey with you.

www.ingramcontent.com/pod-product-compliance
Lightning Source LLC
Chambersburg PA
CBHW071047260726
48661CB00007B/3183